How to Draw a Map

JULIA J. QUINLAN

PowerKiDS press™

New York

Published in 2012 by The Rosen Publishing Group, Inc.
29 East 21st Street, New York, NY 10010

First Edition

Editor: Amelie von Zumbusch
Book Design: Greg Tucker

Photo Credits: Cover Flying Colours Ltd/Getty Images; pp. 4, 10 National Park Service; pp. 5, 8, 9, 14, 15 (top), 20, 22 Shutterstock.com; p. 6 © Map Resources; p. 11 Hemera/Thinkstock; p. 12 Stockbyte/ Thinkstock; pp. 13 (right), 18 GeoAtlas; p. 15 (bottom) Dougal Waters/Digital Vision/Getty Images; p. 19 (left) © www.iStockphoto.com/Mark Rose; p. 21 Marco Garcia/Getty Images.

Library of Congress Cataloging-in-Publication Data

Quinlan, Julia J.
  How to draw a map / by Julia J. Quinlan. — 1st ed.
      p. cm. — (How to use maps)
  Includes index.
  ISBN 978-1-4488-6158-3 (library binding) — ISBN 978-1-4488-6274-0 (pbk.) —
ISBN 978-1-4488-6275-7 (6-pack)
  1. Map drawing—Juvenile literature. I. Title.
  GA130.Q47 2012
  526—dc23
                              2011022768

Manufactured in the United States of America

CPSIA Compliance Information: Batch #WW12PK: For Further Information contact Rosen Publishing, New York, New York at 1-800-237-9932

Contents

Making Maps

Maps are very useful. They can help us find our way and learn about faraway places. People who draw maps are called **cartographers**. Cartographers make all different kinds of maps. There are world maps, **physical maps**, city maps, and more.

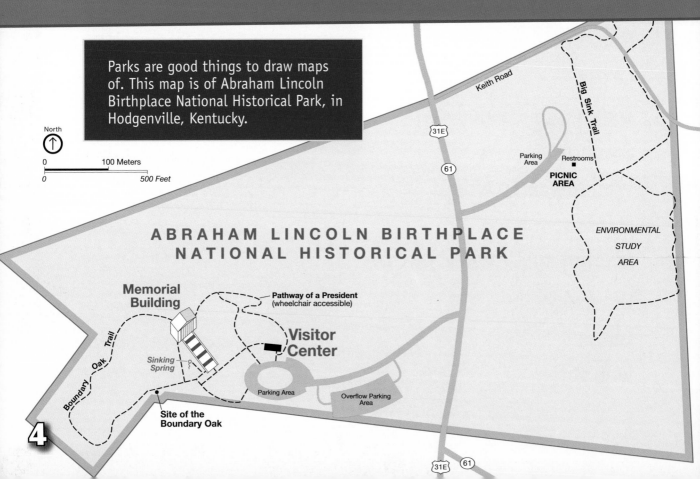

Parks are good things to draw maps of. This map is of Abraham Lincoln Birthplace National Historical Park, in Hodgenville, Kentucky.

North

0   100 Meters
0   500 Feet

Keith Road

Big Sink Trail

31E

61

Parking Area

Restrooms

PICNIC AREA

ENVIRONMENTAL STUDY AREA

A B R A H A M   L I N C O L N   B I R T H P L A C E
N A T I O N A L   H I S T O R I C A L   P A R K

Memorial Building

Pathway of a President
(wheelchair accessible)

Visitor Center

Boundary Oak Trail

Sinking Spring

Parking Area

Overflow Parking Area

Site of the Boundary Oak

31E   61

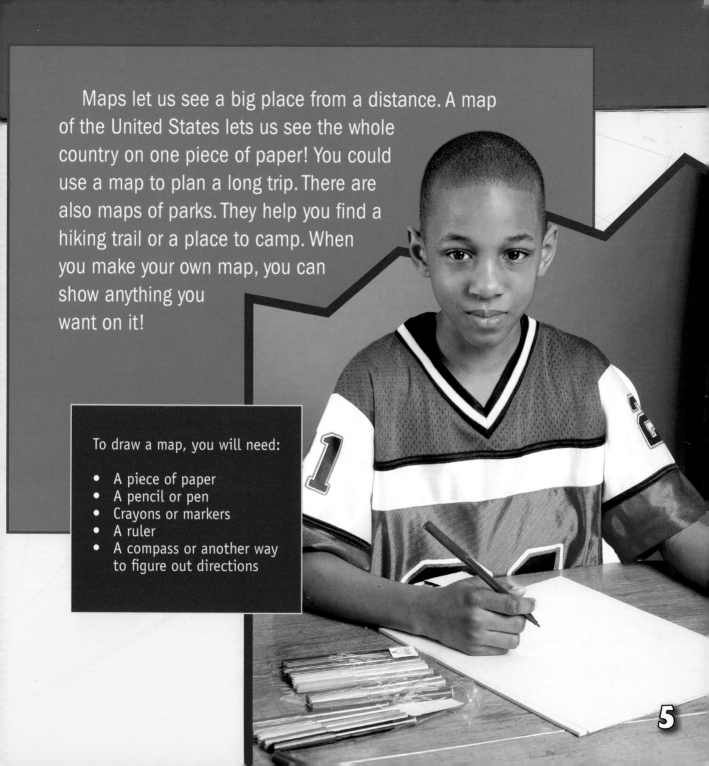

Maps let us see a big place from a distance. A map of the United States lets us see the whole country on one piece of paper! You could use a map to plan a long trip. There are also maps of parks. They help you find a hiking trail or a place to camp. When you make your own map, you can show anything you want on it!

To draw a map, you will need:

- A piece of paper
- A pencil or pen
- Crayons or markers
- A ruler
- A compass or another way to figure out directions

5

What Kind of Map to Draw

Making your own map can be fun. First, you must decide what kind of map you want to draw. You could make a map of your town. You could also make a map of the inside of your house, called a floor plan. If you know a lot about **geography**, you could make a map of your state or even the whole country!

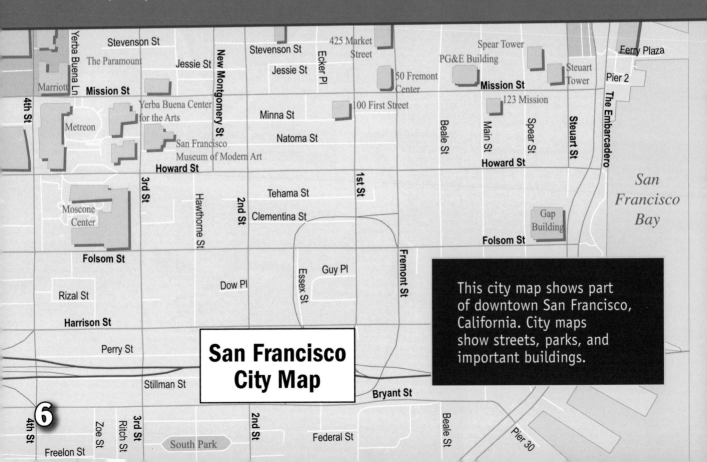

San Francisco City Map

This city map shows part of downtown San Francisco, California. City maps show streets, parks, and important buildings.

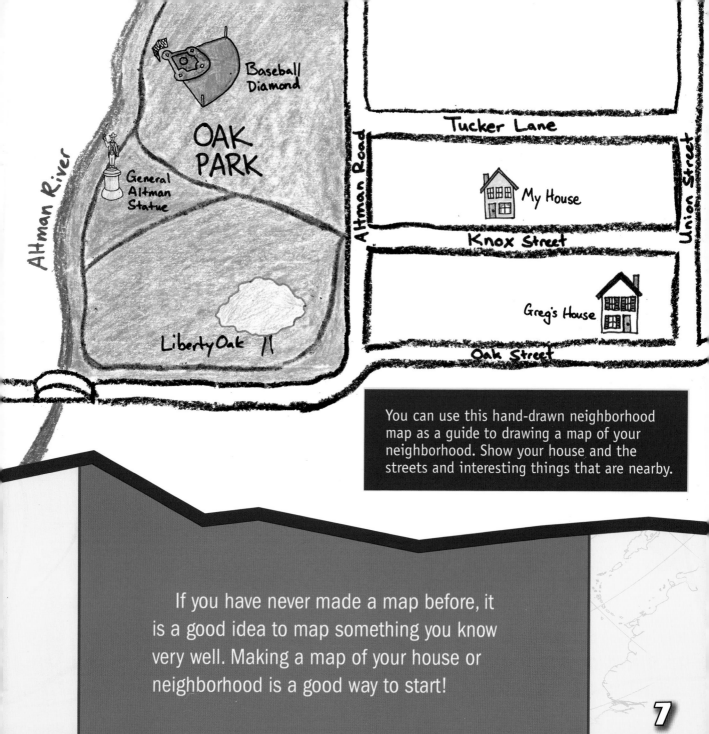

You can use this hand-drawn neighborhood map as a guide to drawing a map of your neighborhood. Show your house and the streets and interesting things that are nearby.

If you have never made a map before, it is a good idea to map something you know very well. Making a map of your house or neighborhood is a good way to start!

Measurement and Distances

If you want your map to show distances correctly, you will need to know how long or far apart things are in real life. You can find this out by taking **measurements**. If you make a floor plan of your house, you can use a tape measure or a ruler to measure the rooms.

This man is measuring a wall with a tape measure. Like rulers, tape measures have inches or centimeters marked off. Unlike rulers, they can be rolled up.

If you want to make a map of your neighborhood, you can ask your parents to drive you around. Most cars count the miles or kilometers as they move. If you want to make a map of a bigger area, such as a state, you can use another map as a guide.

Some roads or trails have signs marking each mile. These signs are useful if you want to know the distances between places you plan to put on your map.

MILE 1

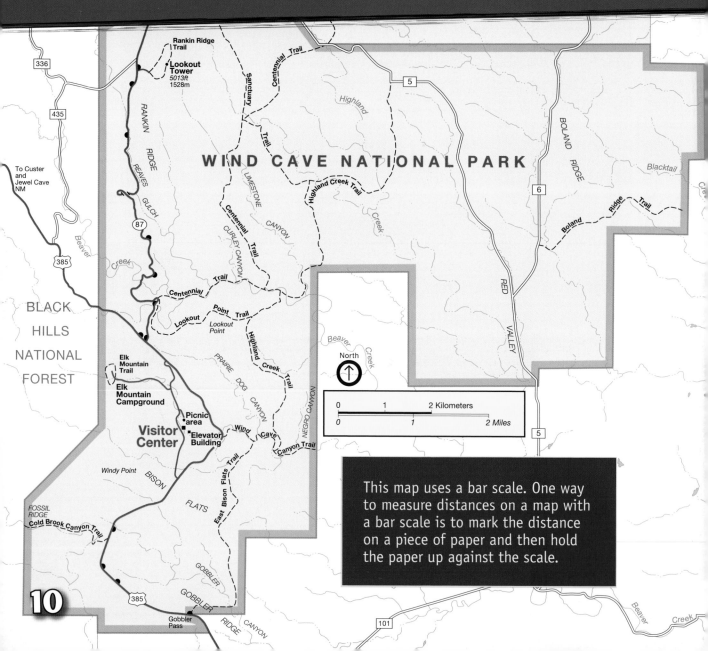

Rankin Ridge Trail

Lookout Tower
5013ft
1528m

336

435

87

385

To Custer and Jewel Cave NM

RANKIN RIDGE

REAVES GULCH

Creek

Beaver

BLACK

HILLS

NATIONAL

FOREST

Sanctuary

Centennial Trail

Trail

LIMESTONE

CANYON

CURLEY CANYON

Centennial Trail

Centennial Trail

Lookout Point Trail

Lookout Point

WIND CAVE NATIONAL PARK

Highland

Highland Creek Trail

Creek

Elk Mountain Trail

Elk Mountain Campground

Picnic area

Visitor Center

Elevator Building

Windy Point

BISON

FLATS

FOSSIL RIDGE

Cold Brook Canyon Trail

PRAIRIE DOG CANYON

Highland Creek Trail

Wind Cave

Canyon Trail

East Bison Flats Trail

NEGRO CANYON

Beaver Creek

North

BOLAND RIDGE

Blacktail

Boland Ridge Trail

RED VALLEY

5

6

Creek

North
↑

0		1		2 Kilometers
0		1		2 Miles

This map uses a bar scale. One way to measure distances on a map with a bar scale is to mark the distance on a piece of paper and then hold the paper up against the scale.

GOBBLER

GOBBLER RIDGE CANYON

Gobbler Pass

385

101

Beaver Creek

Add a **scale** to show the relationship between distances on your map and distances in real life. If a wall in your house is 10 feet (3 m) long, you could make it 2 inches (5 cm) long on your map. Everything on a map should be at the same scale. If another wall is 20 feet (6 m) long, it should be 4 inches (10 cm) on the map.

You can note the scale by writing 2 inches = 10 feet or 5 cm = 3 m. To make a bar scale, use a ruler to draw a line that is 2 inches or 5 cm long. Mark off inches or centimeters on the line and note the distance that each mark stands for.

City maps, such as the one this girl is looking at, have a fairly large scale. Maps that show a bigger area, such as maps of a whole country, have a smaller scale.

Grids

Some maps have grids over them. Grids are made of **horizontal** and **vertical** lines. They divide a map up into squares. Each square has the same area.

You can draw a grid on your map. When you make a grid, it is important to space all your lines evenly so that all the boxes are the same size.

Label the rows and columns on your map with numbers and letters. If a friend asks where something is on your map, you just say the letter and number of the square.

It is a good idea to use a ruler to draw your map grid, as the girl here is doing.

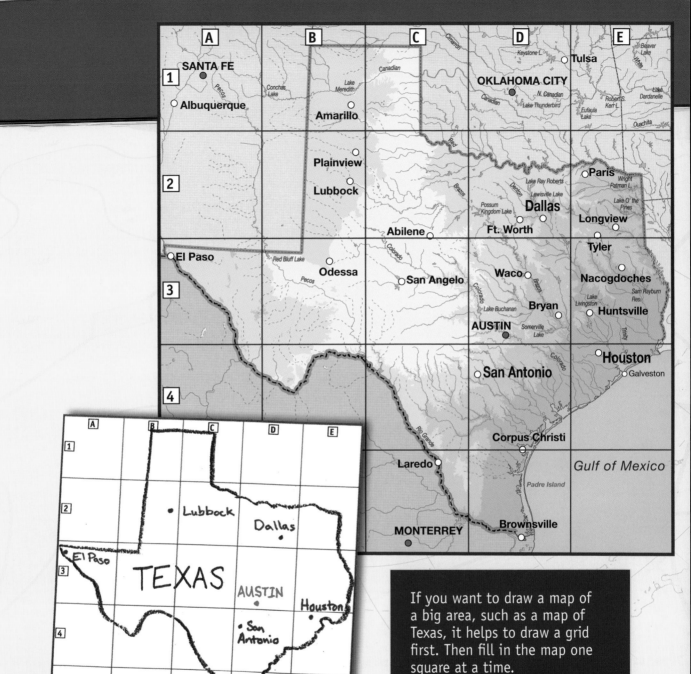

If you want to draw a map of a big area, such as a map of Texas, it helps to draw a grid first. Then fill in the map one square at a time.

13

Bridges, such as this one in New York City's Central Park, are important landmarks. Maps often show bridges on them. See the map on page 16 for an example of this.

Many maps show important places. Important places are called **landmarks**. Landmarks can be helpful when giving directions. You can tell someone to turn right at the post office. Landmarks do not have to be buildings. They can be rivers or roads. If people are visiting your town, they might want to see all of the

landmarks. If you put landmarks on your map, visitors can use it to find them.

When you draw your own map, you can choose which landmarks to include. Your house could be a landmark. A park or even a tree could be a landmark. Choose places that matter to you!

Top: This statue of George Washington riding a horse is in Boston, Massachusetts. A statue is one kind of landmark.
Right: A statue is a great landmark to draw on your map. See page 16 for an example of a statue on a map.

Symbols

Many maps have **symbols**. A symbol is a picture that shows a place or thing. Symbols are often used to show landmarks. On a map of your town, you could show where the supermarket is by putting a picture of a

Maps often have legends that list what the symbols on them mean. To add a legend to your map, draw a box. Inside it, draw each symbol you used on the map. Write what each symbol stands for next to it.

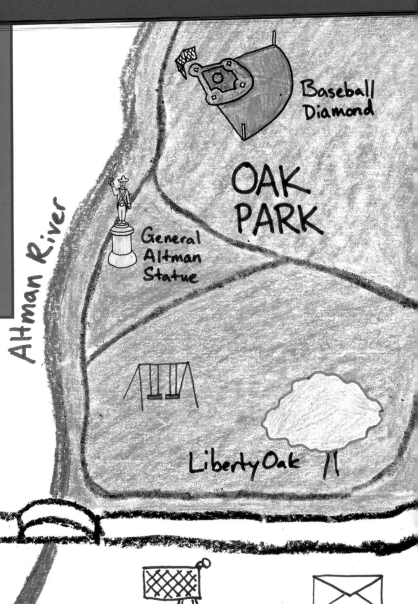

Baseball Diamond

OAK PARK

Altman River

General Altman Statue

Liberty Oak

shopping cart. If you wanted to show where the post office is, you could put a picture of an envelope on your map. To show your house, you could draw a picture of a house!

Draw lines that follow the paths of real-life roads to show roads. You can draw a river with a blue line. You can make a symbol for almost anything!

Tucker Lane

Altman Road

Union Street

 My House

Knox Street

 Greg's House

 Altman Elementary School

Oak Street

Oak Street

LEGEND

	Post Office	/ⅢⅢ\	Playground	——	Trail
📖	Library	～～	River		Traffic Light
	Supermarket	＝＝	Street	⌒	Bridge

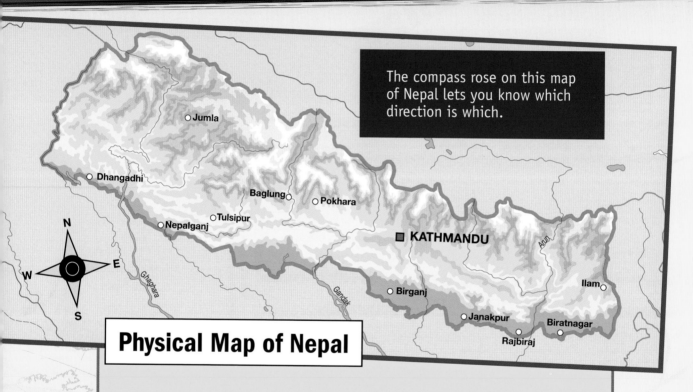

The compass rose on this map of Nepal lets you know which direction is which.

Physical Map of Nepal

Many maps have **compass roses**. A compass rose shows which way north, south, east, and west are on the map. Compass roses may look like stars, with points showing each direction.

If you want a compass rose on your map, you will have to figure out which way is north in real life. To find which way is north, you can look at a compass. If you do not have a compass, you can use another map of the same area. Having a compass rose is important. It helps people match up what they see on a map with what they see on the ground.

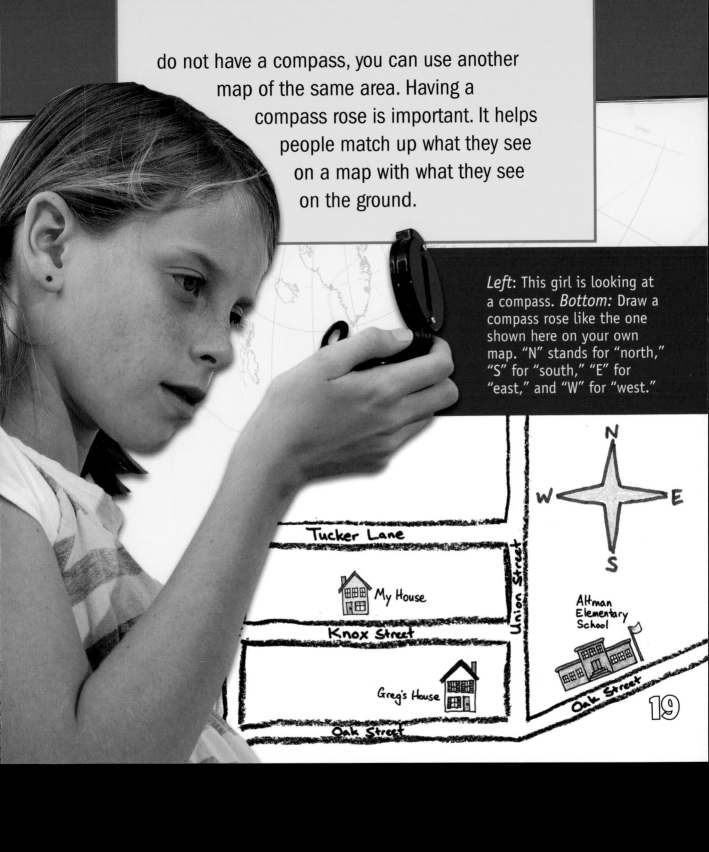

Left: This girl is looking at a compass. *Bottom:* Draw a compass rose like the one shown here on your own map. "N" stands for "north," "S" for "south," "E" for "east," and "W" for "west."

N

W — E

S

Tucker Lane

Union Street

My House

Altman Elementary School

Knox Street

Greg's House

Oak Street

Oak Street

Cartographers

Cartographers have been making maps for thousands of years. In the past, they often had to depend on people to take measurements for them. Now, they have **satellites**, computers, and other **technology**. Satellites take pictures of the world from space. These pictures help cartographers make **accurate** maps.

Even today, cartographers still depend on people for some map measurements. This man is measuring land in Chicago, Illinois, along the shore of Lake Michigan.

Earlier cartographers drew their maps by hand. Some still do this. Many use computers to make maps, though. Cartographers have very important jobs. Governments, scientists, and many other people use the maps they make. Some maps guide people on journeys. Other maps are used to set the borders between countries.

This scientist uses a mix of maps and other tools to track tsunamis in the Pacific Ocean. Tsunamis are huge waves that can cause a lot of damage.

Making Maps Work for You

Adding more information to maps can be fun. You can take a map of your town and add things that are important to you. You can draw symbols to show where your house and your school are. If you know shortcuts, you can add those, too!

There is a lot to remember when making your own map. Compass roses, symbols, and scales are just a few of the things maps need. Once you make your own map, you can use it to find your way!

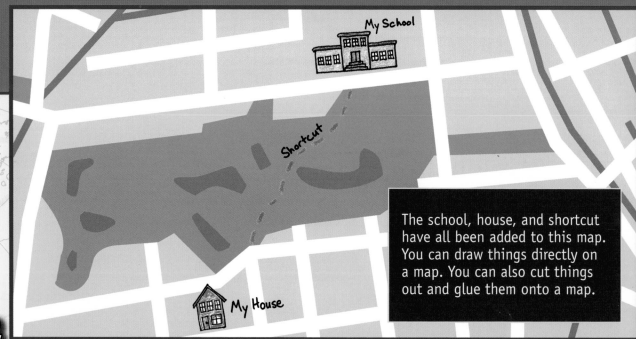

My School

Shortcut

My House

The school, house, and shortcut have all been added to this map. You can draw things directly on a map. You can also cut things out and glue them onto a map.

Glossary

accurate (A-kyuh-rut) Exactly right.

cartographers (kar-TAH-gruh-furz) Mapmakers.

compass roses (KUM-pus ROHZ-ez) Drawings on maps that show directions.

geography (jee-AH-gruh-fee) The study of Earth's weather, land, countries, people, and businesses.

horizontal (hor-ih-ZON-til) Going from side to side.

landmarks (LAND-marks) Buildings or places that are worth noticing.

measurements (MEH-zher-ments) Measures of how long or how far apart things are.

physical maps (FIH-zih-kul MAPS) Maps that show the natural things in a place, such as mountains and rivers.

satellites (SA-tih-lyts) Spacecraft that circle Earth.

scale (SKAYL) The measurements on a map compared to actual measurements on Earth.

symbols (SIM-bulz) Objects or pictures that stand for other things.

technology (tek-NAH-luh-jee) Advanced tools that help people do and make things.

vertical (VER-tih-kul) In an up-and-down direction.

Index

Web Sites

Due to the changing nature of Internet links, PowerKids Press has developed an online list of Web sites related to the subject of this book. This site is updated regularly. Please use this link to access the list:
www.powerkidslinks.com/maps/draw/